Modern lifestyles being so busy and hectic, the advantages of cooking a dish all in one pot are obvious. It saves time and avoids having to use – and clean – numerous saucepans. It is also extremely convenient to cook vegetables or other accompanying ingredients such as pasta along with your chosen meat or fish. A further advantage is that attractive, colourful ovenware or similar cooking vessels can be brought straight to the table, so the pot can double up as a serving dish. Clearly, you will need some back-up saucepans on occasion, if an ingredient has to be cooked prior to being added to the pot, but, as you will see from most of the recipes in this book, the main cooking takes place in just one frying pan, wok, saucepan or casserole.

You can create a variety of dishes, either on the hob or in the oven, using the one-pot method, from soups to Oriental-style stir-fries, pasta or meat-based bakes, pan-fried meats, curries based on both meat and vegetables, risottos, and meat or fish stews of every description. Many are a meal in themselves, needing little accompaniment other than crusty bread, rice or perhaps a crisp green salad.

The most obvious one-pot dish is soup, which, with the addition of pasta, as in Veal & Wild Mushroom Soup with Vermicelli (see page 6) can be hearty enough to serve as a main course. Soup is quick and easy to make; you can sweat your chosen vegetables in a large saucepan, add stock, water or canned tomatoes to the same pan then leave everything to cook while you get on with other tasks.

Wherever possible, it is best to use fresh, home-made stock when making soup because it really makes all the difference to the texture and flavour. Make a large batch of chicken stock when you have the time, using a left-over carcass, some onions, carrots, leeks and celery, a bouquet garni and some peppercorns, strain it to remove all the fat, and freeze it in convenient portions. The soups in this book range from the comforting, such as Cabbage Soup with Sausage (see page 5) to the more exotic, such as Thai Coconut Soup (see page 14), a fragrant blend of chicken and coconut milk spiked with citrus-scented lemon grass, lime leaves, ginger, chilli and coriander, and Clam & Sorrel

Soup (see page 43), in which clams marry with white wine, cream and shredded sorrel to make an elegant, delicately flavoured soup. A chowder recipe is also included (see Fish & Crab Chowder, page 44), a filling soup based on smoked fish, crab, vegetables and rice. Chowders are stew-like soups made with seafood and vegetables, often with the addition of potatoes and milk. The name is derived from the French chaudière, the pot or kettle in which such soups were traditionally cooked.

You can rustle up some very quick dishes using just a frying pan, wok or casserole dish. Vegetarians will love the recipe for Chick Peas & Parma Ham (see page 7), a tempting mixture of Italian cured ham, canned chick peas and red pepper which can be cooked in a matter of minutes, using ingredients you are likely to have on hand in the fridge or store cupboard. Serve this with plenty of crusty bread .The same goes for Greek Beans (see page 26), in which canned haricot beans combine with garlic, chopped red onion and black olives to make an appetizing dish to be served either warm or cold. Pork & Vegetable Stir-Fry (see page 10) is a satisfying, easily prepared combination of lean pork fillet, red pepper, water chestnuts and bean sprouts, flavoured with garlic, ginger and Chinese rice wine and sweetened with a pinch of dark brown sugar.

Meat dishes come into their own prepared the one-pot way. Try Beef & Potato Goulash (see page 12), a perennial favourite, where the potatoes are cooked with the meat in the paprika-flavoured stock; Tomato & Sausage Pan-Fry (see page 11), in which potato slices, broccoli florets and tomato wedges are simmered in red wine and passata with chopped fresh basil, is both quick and easy to prepare and an innovative way to serve those flavoured herb, mustard or leek sausages that are now widely available in supermarkets; or Chicken & Pasta Bake (see page 18), where chicken and raisins and soft cheese flavoured with garlic and herbs are stirred into cooked penne, fennel and mushrooms then topped with slices of mozzarella cheese and baked until golden brown. Quick Chicken Bake (see page 17) is a variation on the classic cottage pie, which uses minced chicken. Topped with creamy mashed potatoes and sprinkled with cheese, it is baked until bubbling. An easy-to-follow recipe for the classic Cajun dish, Jambalaya (see page 50) is also included, an everlasting favourite made with chicken, sausage and prawns.

This book includes a number of fish dishes, some combined with rice, which can be prepared with little fuss. Giant Garlic Prawns (see page 45), stir-fried in olive oil with garlic and chillies until sizzling, are ready within minutes. In Spicy Monkfish Rice (see page 47), firm-textured monkfish is marinated in a spicy paste made with chilli, garlic, saffron, mint and lemon then briskly fried until browned and combined with rice and simmered in coconut milk. The classic fish and rice dish, kedgeree, is given a new twist in Modern Kedgeree (see page 49), which uses both fresh and smoked salmon,

double cream and fresh dill. Italian Fish Stew (see page 51) is a hearty mixture of firm white fish, pasta, courgettes and canned tomatoes. Baked Fresh Sardines (see page 55), flavoured with thyme and sprinkled with Parmesan cheese, make an unusual and delicious main course.

Rice also features as the star ingredient in a number of recipes, notably risottos. Seafood Risotto with Oregano (see page 56), Crab Risotto (see page 57) and Lobster Risotto (see page 59) are all quick and easy to make. Rice with Fruit & Nuts (see page 33) is a filling dish of rice, dried apricots and bananas, spiced with garlic, ginger, chilli and cumin seeds.

Vegetarians need not feel left out! Vegetable Galette (see page 32) is an elegant dish of aubergines and courgettes layered with a quickly prepared fresh tomato sauce and served with a topping of bubbling cheese, and Ratatouille Grill (see page 34) takes the basic Mediterranean recipe, adding diced potatoes on top to turn it into a meal in itself. Potato, Pepper & Mushroom Hash (see page 24) can be adapted to any vegetables you have to hand and Vegetable Toad-in-the-Hole (see page 28), a vegetable bake topped with mustard batter, makes an interesting change. Curry lovers are also catered for, with Potato Curry (see page 38), an irresistible blend of spices including cumin and coriander, Chick Pea Curry (see page 39) and Egg Curry (see page 40), which could be served either as a side dish or light lunch.

Speed and convenience need not mean sacrificing culinary creativity, as the one-pot recipes in this book prove. They are uncomplicated but appetizing, suitable for either entertaining or, more informally, for quick, simple lunch or supper dishes to prepare for the family.

cabbage soup with sausage

Spicy or smoky sausages add substance to this soup, which makes a hearty and warming supper, served with crusty bread and green salad.

Preparation time 10 mins
Cooking time 1¼ hours
Serves 4

Calories 160
Carbohydrate 12 g
Sugars 7 g
Protein 10 g
Fat 8 g
Saturates 2 g

INGREDIENTS

350 g/12 oz lean sausages, preferably
   highly seasoned

2 tsp oil

1 onion, finely chopped

1 leek, halved lengthways and
   thinly sliced

2 carrots, halved and thinly sliced

400 g/14 oz canned chopped tomatoes

350 g/12 oz young green cabbage, cored
   and coarsely shredded

1–2 garlic cloves, finely chopped

pinch of dried thyme

1.5 litres/2¾ pints chicken or meat stock

salt and pepper

freshly grated Parmesan cheese, to serve

1 Put the sausages in water to cover generously and bring to the boil. Reduce the heat and simmer until firm. Drain the sausages and, when cool enough to handle, remove the skin, if you wish, and slice thinly.

2 Heat the oil in a large saucepan over a medium heat, add the onion, leek and carrots and cook for 3–4 minutes, stirring frequently, until the onion starts to soften.

3 Add the tomatoes, cabbage, garlic, thyme, stock and sausages. Bring to the boil, reduce the heat to low and cook gently, partially covered, for about 40 minutes until the vegetables are tender.

4 Taste the soup and adjust the seasoning, if necessary. Ladle into warm bowls and serve with Parmesan cheese.

veal & wild mushroom soup with vermicelli

Wild mushrooms are available commercially and an increasing range of cultivated varieties is now to be found in many supermarkets.

Preparation time 5 mins
Cooking time 3¼ hours
Serves 4

Calories 413
Carbohydrate 28 g
Sugars 3 g
Protein 28 g
Fat 22 g
Saturates 12 g

INGREDIENTS

450 g/1 lb veal, thinly sliced

450 g/1 lb veal bones

1.2 litres/2 pints water

1 small onion

6 peppercorns

1 tsp cloves

pinch of mace

140 g/5 oz oyster and shiitake
   mushrooms, roughly chopped

150 ml/¼ pint double cream

100 g/3½ oz dried vermicelli

1 tbsp cornflour

3 tbsp milk

salt and pepper

1 Put the veal, bones and water in a large saucepan. Bring to the boil and lower the heat. Add the onion, peppercorns, cloves and mace and simmer for about 3 hours, until the veal stock is reduced by one-third.

2 Strain the stock, skim off any fat from the surface with a metal spoon, and pour the stock into a clean saucepan. Add the veal meat to the pan.

3 Add the mushrooms and cream, bring to the boil over a low heat and simmer for 12 minutes. Meanwhile, cook the vermicelli in lightly salted boiling water until just tender, but still firm to the bite. Drain and keep warm.

4 Mix together the cornflour and milk to form a smooth paste. Stir into the soup to thicken. Season to taste with salt and pepper and just before serving, add the vermicelli. Transfer the soup to a warm tureen and serve immediately.

chick peas & parma ham

Prosciutto is a cured ham, which is air- and salt-dried for up to 1 year.

Parma ham is said to be the best of the many varieties available.

Preparation time 10 mins

Cooking time 15 mins

Serves 4

Calories 180

Carbohydrate 18 g

Sugars 2 g

Protein 12 g

Fat 7 g

Saturates 1 g

INGREDIENTS

1 tbsp olive oil

1 medium onion, thinly sliced

1 garlic clove, chopped

1 small red pepper, deseeded and cut
  into thin strips

200 g/7 oz Parma ham, diced

400g/14 oz canned chick peas, drained
  and rinsed

1 tbsp chopped fresh parsley, to garnish

crusty bread, to serve

1 Heat the oil in a frying pan. Add the onion, garlic and pepper and cook over a medium heat, stirring occasionally, for 3–4 minutes or until the vegetables have softened.

2 Add the Parma ham and fry for 5 minutes or until the ham is just beginning to brown.

3 Add the chick peas to the pan and cook, stirring constantly, for about 2–3 minutes until warmed through.

4 Sprinkle with chopped parsley and transfer to warm serving plates. Serve with lots of fresh crusty bread.

rice & peas

If you can get fresh peas – and willing helpers to shell them – do use them: you will need 1 kg/2 lb 4 oz.

Preparation time 10 mins
Cooking time 45 mins
Serves 4

Calories 409
Carbohydrate 38 g
Sugars 2 g
Protein 15 g
Fat 23 g
Saturates 12 g

INGREDIENTS

1 tbsp olive oil

4 tbsp butter

55 g/2 oz pancetta or streaky
   bacon, chopped

1 small onion, chopped

1.4 litres/2½ pints hot chicken stock

200 g/7 oz risotto rice

3 tbsp chopped fresh parsley

225 g/8 oz fresh, frozen or canned
   petits pois

55 g/2 oz grated Parmesan cheese

pepper

1   Heat the olive oil and half of the butter in a heavy-based saucepan. Add the pancetta or bacon and onion and cook over a low heat, stirring occasionally, for 5 minutes until the onion is softened and translucent, but not browned.

2   Add the stock and fresh peas, if using, to the saucepan and bring to the boil. Stir in the rice and season to taste with pepper. Bring to the boil, lower the heat and simmer, stirring occasionally, for 20–30 minutes until the rice is tender. Add the parsley and frozen or canned petit pois and cook for about 8 minutes until the peas are heated through.

3   Stir in the remaining butter and the Parmesan.

4   Transfer to a warmed serving dish and serve immediately, sprinkled with freshly ground black pepper.

pork stroganoff

*Tender, lean pork, cooked in a tasty, rich tomato sauce,
is flavoured with the extra tang of natural yogurt.*

Preparation time 2¼ hours
Cooking time 30 mins
Serves 4

Calories 223
Carbohydrate 12 g
Sugars 7 g
Protein 22 g
Fat 10 g
Saturates 3 g

INGREDIENTS

350 g/12 oz lean pork fillet

1 tbsp vegetable oil

1 medium onion, chopped

2 garlic cloves, crushed

25 g/1 oz plain flour

2 tbsp tomato purée

425 ml/15 fl oz chicken or
    vegetable stock

125 g/4½ oz button mushrooms, sliced

1 large green pepper, deseeded
    and diced

salt and pepper

½ tsp ground nutmeg

4 tbsp low-fat natural yogurt,
    plus extra to serve

boiled white rice, to serve

ground nutmeg, to garnish

1 Trim away any excess fat and membrane from the pork, then cut the meat into slices 1 cm/½ inch thick.

2 Heat the oil in a large saucepan and gently fry the pork, onion and garlic for 4–5 minutes until they are lightly browned.

3 Stir in the flour and tomato purée, pour in the stock and stir to mix thoroughly.

4 Add the mushrooms, green pepper, seasoning and nutmeg. Bring to the boil, cover and simmer for 20 minutes until the pork is tender and cooked through.

5 Remove the saucepan from the heat and then stir in the yogurt.

6 Serve the stroganoff on a bed of rice with an extra spoonful of yogurt, and garnish with a dusting of ground nutmeg.

pork and vegetable stir-fry

This is a very simple dish which lends itself to almost any
combination of vegetables that you have to hand.

Preparation time 5 mins
Cooking time 15 mins
Serves 4

Calories 216
Carbohydrate 5 g
Sugars 3 g
Protein 19 g
Fat 12 g
Saturates 3 g

INGREDIENTS

2 tbsp vegetable oil

2 garlic cloves, crushed

1-cm/½-inch piece of root ginger, cut
    into slivers

350 g/12 oz lean pork fillet, thinly sliced

1 carrot, cut into matchsticks

1 red pepper, deseeded and diced

1 bulb fennel, sliced

25 g/1 oz water chestnuts, halved

85 g/3 oz bean sprouts

2 tbsp Chinese rice wine

300 m/10 fl oz chicken stock

pinch of dark brown sugar

1 tsp cornflour

2 tsp water

1 Heat the oil in a pre-heated wok. Add the garlic, ginger and pork. Stir-fry for
1–2 minutes until the meat is sealed.

2 Add the carrot, pepper, fennel and water chestnuts and stir-fry for 2–3 minutes.
Add the beansprouts and stir-fry for 1 minute. Remove the pork and vegetables, set
aside and keep warm.

3 Add the Chinese rice wine, chicken stock and sugar to the wok. Blend the
cornflour to a smooth paste with the water and stir it into the sauce. Bring to the
boil, stirring constantly until thickened and clear.

4 Return the meat and vegetables to the wok and cook for 1–2 minutes until
heated through and coated with the sauce. Serve immediately.

tomato & sausage pan-fry

This simple dish is delicious as a main meal. Choose good sausages flavoured

with herbs or use flavoured sausages, such as mustard or leek.

Preparation time 5 mins
Cooking time 30 mins
Serves 4

Calories 458
Carbohydrate 34 g
Sugars 11 g
Protein 21 g
Fat 25 g
Saturates 8 g

INGREDIENTS

600 g/1 lb 5 oz potatoes, sliced

1 tbsp vegetable oil

8 flavoured sausages

1 red onion, cut into 8 wedges

1 tbsp tomato purée

150 ml/5 fl oz red wine

150 ml/5 fl oz passata

2 large tomatoes, each cut into 8 wedges

175 g/6 oz broccoli florets, blanched

2 tbsp chopped fresh basil

salt and pepper

shredded fresh basil, to garnish

1   Cook the sliced potatoes in a saucepan of boiling water for 7 minutes. Drain thoroughly and set aside. Meanwhile, heat the oil in a large, heavy-based frying pan. Add the sausages and cook over a medium-low heat for 5 minutes, turning them frequently to ensure that they are browned on all sides.

2   Add the onion pieces to the pan and cook, stirring occasionally, for a further 5 minutes. Stir in the tomato

purée, red wine and passata and mix well. Add the tomato wedges, broccoli florets and chopped basil and mix gently.

3   Add the parboiled potato slices to the pan. Cook the mixture for about 10 minutes or until the sausages and potatoes are completely cooked through. Season to taste with salt and pepper.

4   Transfer to a warmed serving dish, garnish the pan-fry with shredded basil and serve hot.

beef & potato goulash

In this recipe, the potatoes are cooked in the goulash. For a change,
you may prefer to substitute small, scrubbed, new potatoes.

Preparation time 15 mins
Cooking time 2¼ hours
Serves 4

Calories 477
Carbohydrate 36 g
Sugars 11 g
Protein 47 g
Fat 16 g
Saturates 5 g

INGREDIENTS

2 tbsp vegetable oil

1 large onion, sliced

2 garlic cloves, crushed

750 g/1 lb 10 oz lean stewing steak

2 tbsp paprika

400 g/14 oz canned chopped tomatoes

2 tbsp tomato purée

1 large red pepper, deseeded
    and chopped

175 g/6 oz mushrooms, sliced

600 ml/1 pint beef stock

500 g/1 lb 2 oz potatoes, cut into
    large chunks

1 tbsp cornflour

salt and pepper

TO GARNISH

4 tbsp low-fat natural yogurt

paprika

chopped fresh parsley

1 Heat the oil in a large saucepan. Add the onion and garlic and cook over a medium heat, stirring occasionally, for 3–4 minutes until softened.

2 Cut the steak into chunks, add to the saucepan and cook over a high heat for about 3 minutes until browned all over.

3 Lower the heat to medium and stir in the paprika. Add the tomatoes, tomato purée, red pepper and mushrooms. Cook, stirring constantly, for 2 minutes.

4 Pour in the beef stock. Bring to the boil, stirring occasionally, then reduce the heat to low. Cover and simmer gently for about 1½ hours until the meat is cooked through and tender.

5 Add the potatoes, cover and cook for a further 20–30 minutes until tender.

6 Blend the cornflour with a little water and add to the pan, stirring until thickened and blended. Cook for 1 minute then season with salt and pepper to taste. Top with the yogurt, sprinkle over the paprika and chopped fresh parsley and serve.

chicken & rice soup

Leftover cooked rice is a handy addition to soups. Any kind of rice is suitable

for this soup – white or brown long-grain rice, or even wild rice.

Preparation time 5 mins
Cooking time 25 mins
Serves 4

Calories 165
Carbohydrate 19 g
Sugars 2 g
Protein 14 g
Fat 4 g
Saturates 1 g

INGREDIENTS

1.5 litres/2¾ pints chicken stock

2 small carrots, very thinly sliced

1 celery stick, finely diced

1 baby leek, halved lengthways and
   thinly sliced

115 g/4 oz petits pois, thawed if frozen

175 g/6 oz cooked rice

150 g/5½ oz cooked chicken meat, sliced

2 tsp chopped fresh tarragon

1 tbsp chopped fresh parsley

salt and pepper

sprigs of fresh parsley, to garnish

crusty bread, to serve

1 Put the chicken stock in a large saucepan and add the carrots, celery and leek. Bring to the boil, reduce the heat to low, partially cover and simmer gently for 10 minutes until the vegetables are tender.

2 Stir in the petits pois, rice and chicken meat and continue cooking for a further 10–15 minutes or until the vegetables are tender.

3 Add the chopped tarragon and parsley and season to taste with salt and pepper.

4 Ladle the soup into warmed bowls, garnish with fresh parsley sprigs and serve immediately with crusty bread.

thai coconut soup

This soup makes a change from traditional chicken soup. It is spicy, and garnished with a generous quantity of fresh coriander leaves.

Preparation time 5 mins
Cooking time 40 mins
Serves 4

Calories 76
Carbohydrate 3 g
Sugars 2 g
Protein 13 g
Fat 1 g
Saturates 0 g

INGREDIENTS

1.2 litres/2 pints chicken stock

2 skinless, boneless chicken breasts

1 fresh chilli, split lengthways
    and deseeded

7.5-cm/3-inch piece lemon grass,
    split lengthways

3–4 lime leaves

2.5-cm/1-inch piece root ginger, peeled
    and sliced

120 ml/4 fl oz coconut milk

6–8 spring onions, sliced diagonally

¼ tsp chilli purée, to taste

salt

fresh coriander leaves, to garnish

1 Put the stock in a saucepan with the chicken, chilli, lemon grass, lime leaves and ginger. Bring almost to the boil, reduce the heat, cover and simmer for 20–25 minutes, or until the chicken is cooked through and firm to the touch.

2 Remove the chicken from the saucepan and strain the stock. When the chicken is cool, slice thinly or chop into bite-sized pieces.

3 Return the stock to the saucepan and heat to simmering. Stir in the coconut milk and spring onions. Add the chicken and continue simmering for about 10 minutes, or until the soup is heated through and the flavours have mingled.

4 Stir in the chilli purée. Season to taste with salt and, if wished, add a little more chilli purée.

5 Ladle into warm bowls and float coriander leaves on top.

toad-in-the-hole

This unusual recipe uses chicken and Cumberland sausage,

which is then made into individual bite-sized cakes.

Preparation time 1¼ hours
Cooking time 30 mins
Serves 4–6

Calories 470
Carbohydrate 30 g
Sugars 4 g
Protein 28 g
Fat 27 g
Saturates 12 g

INGREDIENTS

125 g/4½ oz plain flour

pinch of salt

1 egg, beaten

200 ml/7 fl oz milk

75 ml/3 fl oz water

2 tbsp beef dripping

250 g/9 oz chicken breasts, sliced

250 g/9 oz Cumberland sausage, cut into
    large chunks

chicken or onion gravy, to

    serve (optional)

1 Mix the flour and salt in a bowl, make a well in the centre and add the beaten egg.

2 Add half the milk and slowly work in the flour. Beat until smooth, then add the remaining milk and water. Beat again until smooth. Leave to stand for at least 1 hour.

3 Add the dripping to a large baking tin. Add the chicken and sausage. Heat in a pre-heated oven, at 220°C/425°F/Gas Mark 7, for 5 minutes. Remove from the oven and pour in the batter. Return to the oven to cook for 35 minutes, until risen and golden brown. Do not open the oven door for at least 30 minutes. Serve hot, with gravy, or alone.

peppered chicken stir-fry

Crushed mixed peppercorns coat tender, thin strips of chicken which are cooked with green and red peppers for a really colourful dish.

Preparation time 5 mins
Cooking time 15 mins
Serves 4

Calories 219
Carbohydrate 11 g
Sugars 6 g
Protein 22 g
Fat 10 g
Saturates 2 g

INGREDIENTS

2 tbsp tomato ketchup

2 tbsp soy sauce

450 g/1 lb skinless, boneless,
   chicken breasts

2 tbsp crushed mixed peppercorns

2 tbsp sunflower oil

1 red pepper

1 green pepper

175 g/6 oz sugar snap peas

2 tbsp oyster sauce

1 Mix the tomato ketchup with the soy sauce in a bowl.

2 Using a sharp knife, slice the chicken into thin strips. Toss the chicken in the tomato ketchup and soy sauce mixture. Sprinkle the crushed peppercorns on to a plate. Dip the coated chicken in the peppercorns until evenly coated.

3 Heat the sunflower oil in a pre-heated wok. Add the chicken to the wok and stir-fry for 5 minutes.

4 Deseed and slice the peppers.

5 Add the peppers to the wok together with the sugar snap peas and stir-fry for a further 5 minutes.

6 Add the oyster sauce and allow to bubble for 2 minutes. Transfer to serving bowls and serve immediately.

quick chicken bake

This recipe is a type of cottage pie and is just as versatile. Add vegetables and herbs of your choice, depending on what you have to hand.

Preparation time 1¼ hours
Cooking time 40 mins
Serves 4

Calories 530
Carbohydrate 48 g
Sugars 8 g
Protein 37 g
Fat 23 g
Saturates 12 g

INGREDIENTS

500 g/1lb 2 oz minced chicken

1 large onion, finely chopped

2 carrots, finely diced

25 g/1 oz plain flour

1 tbsp tomato purée

300 ml/10 fl oz chicken stock

salt and pepper

pinch of fresh thyme

900 g/2 lb boiled potatoes, mashed with
    butter and milk and highly seasoned

85 g/3 oz grated Lancashire cheese

peas, to serve

1 Dry-fry the minced chicken, onion and carrots in a non-stick saucepan over a low heat, stirring frequently, for about 5 minutes until the chicken has lost its pink colour. Sprinkle the chicken with the flour and cook, stirring constantly, for a further 2 minutes. Gradually blend in the tomato purée and stock, then simmer for about 15 minutes. Season to taste with salt and pepper and add the thyme.

2 Transfer the chicken and vegetable mixture to an ovenproof dish and set aside to cool completely.

3 Spoon the mashed potatoes over the chicken mixture and sprinkle with the Lancashire cheese. Bake in a pre-heated oven, at 200°C/400°F/Gas Mark 6, for about 20 minutes, or until the cheese is bubbling and golden. Serve with the peas.

chicken & pasta bake

Tender lean chicken is baked with pasta in a creamy low-fat sauce that contrasts well with the fennel and the sweetness of the raisins.

Preparation time 15 mins
Cooking time 45 mins
Serves 4

Calories 380
Carbohydrate 27 g
Sugars 15 g
Protein 39 g
Fat 14 g
Saturates 6 g

INGREDIENTS

2 bulbs fennel

2 red onions, very thinly sliced

1 tbsp lemon juice

125 g/4½ oz button mushrooms

1 tbsp olive oil

salt and pepper

225 g/8 oz dried penne

55 g/2oz raisins

225 g/8 oz skinless, boneless cooked
   chicken, cut into strips

375 g/13 oz low-fat soft cheese with
   garlic and herbs

125 g/4½ oz low-fat mozzarella cheese,
   thinly sliced

35 g/1¼ oz freshly grated
   Parmesan cheese

chopped fennel fronds, to garnish

1 Trim the fennel, reserving the green fronds, and slice the bulbs thinly.

2 Generously coat the onions in the lemon juice. Quarter the mushrooms.

3 Heat the oil in a large frying pan and fry the fennel, onion and mushrooms for 4–5 minutes, stirring, until just softened. Season well, transfer the mixture to a large bowl and set aside.

4 Bring a pan of lightly salted water to the boil and cook the penne according to the instructions on the packet until just cooked. Drain and mix the pasta with the vegetables.

5 Stir the raisins and chicken into the pasta mixture. Soften the soft cheese by beating it, then mix into the pasta and chicken – the heat from the pasta should make the cheese melt slightly.

6 Put the mixture into an ovenproof dish and place on a baking tray. Arrange slices of mozzarella over the top and sprinkle with the grated Parmesan.

7 Bake in a pre-heated oven, at 200°C/400°F/Gas Mark 6, for 20–25 minutes until golden brown.

8 Garnish with chopped fennel fronds and serve hot.

golden chicken pilau

This is a simple version of a creamy and mildly spiced Indian pilau. There are many ingredients, but very little preparation is needed for this dish.

Preparation time 10 mins
Cooking time 20 mins
Serves 4

Calories 581
Carbohydrate 73 g
Sugars 22 g
Protein 31 g
Fat 19 g
Saturates 12 g

INGREDIENTS

4 tbsp butter

8 skinless, boneless chicken thighs,
    cut into large pieces

1 onion, sliced

1 tsp ground turmeric

1 tsp ground cinnamon

250 g/9 oz long-grain rice

salt and pepper

425 ml/15 fl oz natural yogurt

60 g/2¼ oz sultanas

200 ml/7 fl oz chicken stock

1 tomato, chopped

2 tbsp chopped fresh coriander
    or parsley

2 tbsp desiccated coconut, toasted

fresh coriander, to garnish

1   Heat the butter in a heavy or non-stick frying pan and fry the chicken with the onion for about 3 minutes.

2   Stir in the turmeric, cinnamon, rice and seasoning and fry gently for 3 minutes.

3   Add the natural yogurt, sultanas and chicken stock and mix well. Cover and simmer for 10 minutes, stirring occasionally until the rice is tender and all the chicken stock has been absorbed. Add more stock if the mixture becomes too dry.

4   Stir in the chopped tomato and coriander or parsley. Season to taste.

5   Sprinkle the pilau with the toasted coconut and garnish with coriander.

coconut chicken

This tasty Thai-style dish has a classic sauce of lime, peanut, coconut and chilli. You'll find coconut cream in most supermarkets or delicatessens.

Preparation time 5 mins
Cooking time 15 mins
Serves 4

Calories 348
Carbohydrate 3 g
Sugars 2 g
Protein 36 g
Fat 21 g
Saturates 8 g

INGREDIENTS

150 ml/¼ pint hot chicken stock

30 g/1 oz coconut cream

1 tbsp sunflower oil

8 skinless, boneless chicken thighs,
    cut into long, thin strips

1 small red chilli, thinly sliced

4 spring onions, thinly sliced

4 tbsp smooth or crunchy peanut butter

finely grated rind and juice of 1 lime

boiled rice, to serve

spring onion flower and red chilli,
    to garnish

1 Place the chicken stock in a measuring jug and crumble the creamed coconut into it, stirring to dissolve.

2 Heat the oil in a wok or large, heavy-based frying pan and cook the chicken strips, stirring, until golden. Add the sliced red chilli and spring onions to the pan and cook gently for a few minutes, stirring to mix all the ingredients.

3 Add the peanut butter, coconut mixture, lime rind and juice and simmer uncovered, stirring, for about 5 minutes.

4 Serve with boiled rice, garnished with a spring onion flower and a red chilli.

indian potato & pea soup

Garam masala, chilli, cumin and coriander gives this soup a slightly hot and spicy Indian flavour.

Preparation time 5 mins
Cooking time 35 mins
Serves 4

Calories 160
Carbohydrate 21 g
Sugars 8 g
Protein 6 g
Fat 7 g
Saturates 1 g

INGREDIENTS

2 tbsp vegetable oil

225 g/8 oz floury potatoes, diced

1 large onion, chopped

2 garlic cloves, crushed

1 tsp garam masala

1 tsp ground coriander

1 tsp ground cumin

900 ml/1½ pints vegetable stock

1 red chilli, chopped

100 g/3½ oz frozen peas

4 tbsp natural yogurt

salt and pepper

chopped fresh coriander,
   to garnish

1 Heat the vegetable oil in a large saucepan and add the diced potatoes, onion and garlic. Sauté gently for about 5 minutes, stirring constantly. Add the ground spices and cook for 1 minute, stirring all the time.

2 Stir in the vegetable stock and chopped red chilli and bring the mixture to the boil. Reduce the heat, cover the pan and simmer for 20 minutes until the potatoes begin to break down.

3 Add the peas and cook for a further 5 minutes. Stir in the yogurt and season to taste.

4 Pour into warmed soup bowls, garnish with chopped fresh coriander and serve hot with warm bread.

cheese and vegetable chowder

This hearty soup is wonderful made in the middle of winter with fresh seasonal vegetables. Use a really well-flavoured mature Cheddar cheese.

Preparation time 15 mins
Cooking time 45 mins
Serves 4

Calories 669
Carbohydrate 33 g
Sugars 13 g
Protein 26 g
Fat 49 g
Saturates 30 g

INGREDIENTS

25 g/1 oz butter

1 large onion, finely chopped

1 large leek, split lengthways and
    thinly sliced

1–2 garlic cloves, crushed

55 g/2 oz plain flour

1.2 litres/2 pints vegetable stock

3 carrots, finely diced

2 celery sticks, finely diced

1 turnip, finely diced

1 large potato, finely diced

3–4 sprigs fresh thyme or ⅛ tsp
    dried thyme

1 bay leaf

350 ml/12 fl oz single cream

300 g/10½ oz mature Cheddar
    cheese, grated

chopped fresh parsley, to garnish

salt and pepper

1   Melt the butter in a large, heavy-based saucepan over a medium-low heat. Add the onion, leek and garlic. Cover and cook for about 5 minutes, stirring frequently, until the vegetables are starting to soften.

2   Stir the flour into the vegetables and continue cooking for 2 minutes. Add a little of the stock and stir well, scraping the bottom of the pan to mix in the flour. Bring to the boil, stirring frequently, and slowly stir in the rest of the stock.

3   Add the carrots, celery, turnip, potato, thyme and bay leaf. Reduce the heat, cover the pan and cook the soup gently for about 35 minutes, stirring occasionally, until the vegetables are tender. Remove the bay leaf and the thyme sprigs.

4   Stir in the cream and simmer over a very low heat for 5 minutes.

5   Add the cheese, a handful at a time, stirring constantly for 1 minute after each addition to make sure it is completely melted. Adjust the seasoning.

6   Ladle the soup immediately into warm bowls, sprinkle with parsley and serve.

onions à la grecque

This well-known method of cooking vegetables is perfect for shallots

or onions. Serve them with a crisp salad and chunks of bread.

Preparation time 10 mins
Cooking time 15 mins
Serves 4

Calories 200
Carbohydrate 28 g
Sugars 26 g
Protein 2 g
Fat 9 g
Saturates 1 g

INGREDIENTS

450 g/1 lb shallots

3 tbsp olive oil

3 tbsp clear honey

2 tbsp garlic wine vinegar

3 tbsp dry white wine

1 tbsp tomato purée

2 celery sticks, sliced

2 tomatoes, deseeded and chopped

salt and pepper

chopped celery leaves, to garnish

1 Peel the shallots. Heat the oil in a large saucepan, add the shallots and cook, stirring, for 3–5 minutes, or until they begin to brown.

2 Add the honey and cook over a high heat for a further 30 seconds, then add the garlic wine vinegar and dry white wine, stirring well.

3 Stir in the tomato purée, the celery and the tomatoes, and bring the mixture to the boil. Cook over a high heat for 5–6 minutes. Season to taste and leave to cool slightly.

4 Garnish with chopped celery leaves and serve warm. Alternatively, chill in the refrigerator before serving.

potato, pepper & mushroom hash

This dish is ideal for a quick snack. Packed with colour and flavour, it is very versatile and you can add any other vegetable you have to hand.

Preparation time 10 mins
Cooking time 35 mins
Serves 4

Calories 378
Carbohydrate 20 g
Sugars 14 g
Protein 18 g
Fat 26 g
Saturates 7 g

INGREDIENTS

675 g/1½ lb potatoes, cubed

1 tbsp olive oil

2 garlic cloves, crushed

1 green pepper, cubed

1 yellow pepper, cubed

3 tomatoes, diced

75 g/2¾ oz button mushrooms, halved

1 tbsp Worcestershire sauce

2 tbsp chopped basil

salt and pepper

sprigs of fresh basil, to garnish

crusty bread, to serve

1 Cook the potatoes in a saucepan of boiling salted water for 7–8 minutes. Drain well and reserve. Heat the oil in a large, heavy-based frying pan and cook the potatoes for 8–10 minutes, stirring until browned. Add the garlic and peppers and cook for 2–3 minutes.

2 Stir in the tomatoes and mushrooms and cook, stirring, for 5–6 minutes.

3 Stir in the Worcestershire sauce and basil and season well. Garnish and serve with crusty bread.

carrot & orange bake

Poppy seeds add texture and flavour to this recipe and counteract the slightly sweet flavour of the carrots.

Preparation time 20 mins
Cooking time 40 mins
Serves 4

Calories 138
Carbohydrate 32 g
Sugars 31 g
Protein 2 g
Fat 1 g
Saturates 0.2 g

INGREDIENTS

675 g/1½ lb carrots, cut into matchsticks

1 leek, sliced

300 ml/½ pint fresh orange juice

2 tbsp clear honey

1 garlic clove, crushed

1 tsp mixed spice

2 tsp chopped thyme

salt and pepper

1 tbsp poppy seeds

TO GARNISH

sprigs of fresh thyme

strips of orange rind

1 Cook the carrots and leek in a saucepan of boiling lightly salted water for 5–6 minutes. Drain well and transfer to a shallow ovenproof dish until required.

2 Mix together the orange juice, honey, garlic, mixed spice and thyme and pour the mixture over the vegetables. Season with salt and pepper to taste.

3 Cover the dish and cook in a pre-heated oven, at 180°C/350°F/Gas Mark 4, for 30 minutes, or until the vegetables are tender.

4 Remove the lid and sprinkle with poppy seeds. Garnish with the fresh thyme sprigs and strips of orange rind and serve immediately.

greek beans

This flavoursome dish contains many typically Greek flavours, such as lemon, garlic, oregano and olives.

Preparation time 5 mins
Cooking time 1 hour
Serves 4

Calories 115
Carbohydrate 15 g
Sugars 4 g
Protein 6 g
Fat 4 g
Saturates 0.6 g

INGREDIENTS

400 g/14 oz canned haricot
   beans, drained

1 tbsp olive oil

3 garlic cloves, crushed

425 ml/¾ pint vegetable stock

1 bay leaf

2 sprigs of fresh oregano

1 tbsp tomato purée

juice of 1 lemon

1 small red onion, chopped

25 g/1 oz stoned black olives, halved

salt and pepper

1 Put the haricot beans in a flameproof casserole dish. Add the olive oil and crushed garlic and cook over a gentle heat, stirring occasionally, for 4–5 minutes.

2 Add the stock, bay leaf, oregano, tomato purée, lemon juice and red onion. Cover and simmer for about 1 hour or until the sauce has thickened.

3 Stir in the black olives, then season the beans with salt and pepper to taste. Serve either warm or cold.

spiced mixed vegetables

This is a very popular vegetarian recipe. You can make it with any

vegetables you choose, but the combination below is excellent.

Preparation time 5 mins
Cooking time 45 mins
Serves 4

Calories 669
Carbohydrate 36 g
Sugars 17 g
Protein 7 g
Fat 57 g
Saturates 8 g

INGREDIENTS

vegetable oil, for frying

1 tsp mustard seeds

1 tsp onion seeds

½ tsp white cumin seeds

3–4 curry leaves, chopped

450 g/1 lb onions, finely chopped

3 tomatoes, chopped

½ red and ½ green pepper, sliced

1 tsp finely chopped root ginger

1 tsp crushed fresh garlic

1 tsp chilli powder

¼ tsp turmeric

1 tsp salt

425 ml/15 fl oz water

450 g/1 lb potatoes, cut into pieces

½ cauliflower, cut into small florets

4 carrots, peeled and sliced

3 green chillies, finely chopped

1 tbsp fresh coriander leaves

1 tbsp lemon juice

1 Heat the oil in a large saucepan. Add the mustard, onion and white cumin seeds along with the curry leaves and fry until they turn a shade darker.

2 Add the onions to the pan and fry them over a medium heat until they turn golden brown.

3 Add the tomatoes and peppers and stir-fry for approximately 5 minutes.

4 Add the ginger, garlic, chilli powder, turmeric and salt and mix well.

5 Add 300 ml/10 fl oz of the water, cover the pan and leave to simmer for 10–12 minutes, stirring occasionally.

6 Add the potatoes, cauliflower florets, carrots, green chillies and fresh coriander leaves and cook, stirring, for about 5 minutes.

7 Add the remaining water and the lemon juice to the pan, stirring to combine. Cover the pan and leave the mixture to simmer for about 15 minutes, stirring occasionally, until all the vegtables are cooked.

8 Transfer the mixed vegetables to serving plates and serve immediately.

vegetable toad-in-the-hole

This dish can be cooked in a single large dish or in four individual Yorkshire pudding tins.

Preparation time 15 mins
Cooking time 55 mins
Serves 4

Calories 313
Carbohydrate 31 g
Sugars 9 g
Protein 9 g
Fat 18 g
Saturates 7 g

INGREDIENTS

BATTER

100 g/3½ oz plain flour

2 eggs, beaten

200 ml/7 fl oz milk

2 tbsp wholegrain mustard

2 tbsp vegetable oil

FILLING

25 g/1 oz butter

2 garlic cloves, crushed

1 onion, cut into eight

75 g/2¾ oz baby carrots,
    halved lengthways

50 g/1¾ oz French beans

50 g/1¾ oz canned sweetcorn, drained

2 tomatoes, deseeded and cut
    into chunks

1 tsp wholegrain mustard

1 tbsp chopped mixed herbs

salt and pepper

1 To make the batter, sift the flour and a pinch of salt into a bowl. Beat in the eggs and milk to make a batter. Stir in the mustard and leave to stand.

2 Pour the oil into a shallow ovenproof dish and heat in a pre-heated oven, at 200°C/400°F/Gas Mark 6, for 10 minutes.

3 To make the filling, melt the butter in a frying pan and sauté the garlic and onion, stirring constantly, for 2 minutes. Cook the carrots and beans in a saucepan of boiling water for 7 minutes, or until tender. Drain well.

4 Add the sweetcorn and tomatoes to the frying pan with the mustard and chopped mixed herbs. Season well and add the carrots and beans.

5 Remove the heated dish from the oven and pour in the batter. Spoon the vegetables into the centre, return to the oven and cook for 30–35 minutes, until the batter has risen and set. Serve the vegetable toad-in-the-hole immediately.

potato-topped vegetable pie

This is a very colourful and nutritious dish, packed full of crunchy vegetables in a tasty white wine sauce.

Preparation time 20 mins
Cooking time 1¼ hours
Serves 4

Calories 413
Carbohydrate 41 g
Sugars 11 g
Protein 19 g
Fat 18 g
Saturates 11 g

INGREDIENTS

1 carrot, diced

175 g/6 oz cauliflower florets

175 g/6 oz broccoli florets

1 bulb fennel, sliced

85 g/3 oz French beans, halved

2 tbsp butter

2½ tbsp plain flour

150 ml/5 fl oz vegetable stock

150 ml/5 fl oz dry white wine

150 ml/5 fl oz milk

175 g/6 oz chestnut
  mushrooms, quartered

2 tbsp chopped fresh sage

TOPPING

900 g/2 lb floury potatoes, diced

2 tbsp butter

4 tbsp natural yogurt

70 g/2½ oz Parmesan cheese,
  freshly grated

1 tsp fennel seeds

salt and pepper

1 Cook the carrot, cauliflower, broccoli, fennel and beans in a large saucepan of boiling water for 10 minutes until just tender. Drain the vegetables and set aside.

2 Melt the butter in a saucepan. Stir in the flour and cook, stirring, for 1 minute. Remove from the heat and gradually stir in the stock, wine and milk. Return to the heat and bring to the boil, stirring. Simmer until thickened. Stir in the reserved vegetables, mushrooms and sage.

3 Meanwhile, make the topping. Cook the potatoes in boiling water for 10–15 minutes. Drain and mash with the butter, yogurt and half the cheese. Stir in the fennel seeds. Season to taste.

4 Spoon the vegetable mixture into a 1-litre/1¾-pint pie dish. Spread the potato over the top and sprinkle with the remaining cheese. Cook in a pre-heated oven, at 190°C/375°F/Gas Mark 5, for 30–35 minutes or until golden. Serve hot.

layered potato cake

This tasty meal is made with sliced potatoes, tofu and vegetables,
served from the pan in which they are cooked.

Preparation time 15 mins
Cooking time 30 mins
Serves 4

Calories 452
Carbohydrate 35 g
Sugars 6 g
Protein 17 g
Fat 28 g
Saturates 13 g

INGREDIENTS

675 g/1 lb 8 oz waxy potatoes,
    unpeeled and sliced

1 carrot, diced

225 g/8 oz small broccoli florets

5 tbsp butter

2 tbsp vegetable oil

1 red onion, quartered

2 garlic cloves, crushed

175 g/6 oz firm tofu, diced

2 tbsp chopped fresh sage

85 g/3 oz mature cheese, grated

1 Cook the sliced potatoes in a large saucepan of boiling water for 10 minutes. Drain thoroughly. Meanwhile, cook the carrot and broccoli florets in a separate pan of boiling water for 5 minutes. Remove with a slotted spoon.

2 Heat the butter and oil in a 23-cm/9-inch frying pan. Add the onion and garlic and fry over a low heat for 2–3 minutes. Add half of the potato slices, covering the base of the pan. Cover the potato slices with the carrot, broccoli and tofu. Sprinkle with half of the sage.

3 Cover with the remaining potato slices. Sprinkle the grated cheese over the top.

4 Cook over a moderate heat for 8–10 minutes. Then place the pan under a pre-heated medium grill for about 2–3 minutes, or until the cheese melts and browns.

5 Garnish with the remaining chopped sage and serve immediately, straight from the pan.

vegetarian bean pot

This tasty vegetable, mycoprotein and bean casserole is cooked conventionally,
but can be kept hot over the barbecue to serve as part of a barbecued meal.

Preparation time 10 mins
Cooking time 1 hour
Serves 4

Calories 381
Carbohydrate 34 g
Sugars 17 g
Protein 21 g
Fat 19 g
Saturates 3 g

INGREDIENTS

4 tbsp butter or margarine

1 large onion, chopped

2 garlic cloves, crushed

2 carrots, sliced

2 celery sticks, sliced

1 tbsp paprika

2 tsp ground cumin

400 g/14 oz canned chopped tomatoes

425 g/15 oz canned mixed beans, rinsed
   and drained

150 ml/5 fl oz vegetable stock

1 tbsp muscovado sugar or black treacle

350 g/12 oz mycoprotein or soya cubes

salt and pepper

crusty French bread, to serve

1 Melt the butter or margarine in a large, flameproof casserole and cook the onion and garlic over a medium heat, stirring occasionally, for about 5 minutes, until golden brown.

2 Add the carrots and celery and cook, stirring occasionally, for a further 2 minutes, then stir in the paprika and ground cumin.

3 Add the tomatoes and beans. Pour in the stock and add the sugar or treacle. Bring to the boil, then reduce the heat and simmer, uncovered, stirring occasionally, for 30 minutes.

4 Add the mycoprotein or soya cubes to the casserole, cover and cook, stirring occasionally, for a further 20 minutes.

5 Season to taste with salt and pepper. Keep the casserole hot on the barbecue, if required.

6 Ladle on to plates and serve with crusty French bread.

vegetable galette

This is a simply scrumptious dish of aubergines and courgettes layered with a quick tomato sauce and melted cheese.

Preparation time 40 mins

Cooking time 1¼ hours

Serves 4

Calories 412

Carbohydrate 13 g

Sugars 12 g

Protein 13 g

Fat 34 g

Saturates 11 g

INGREDIENTS

2 large aubergines, sliced

4 courgettes, sliced

800g/1lb 12 oz canned chopped
   tomatoes, drained

2 tbsp tomato purée

2 garlic cloves, crushed

4 tbsp olive oil

1 tsp caster sugar

2 tbsp chopped fresh basil

olive oil, for frying

225 g/8 oz mozzarella cheese, sliced

salt and pepper

fresh basil leaves, to garnish

1 Put the aubergine slices in a colander and sprinkle generously with salt. Set aside for 30 minutes, then rinse well under cold running water and drain. Thinly slice the courgettes. Meanwhile, put the tomatoes, tomato purée, garlic, olive oil, sugar and chopped basil into a pan and simmer for 20 minutes or until reduced by half. Season to taste with salt and pepper.

2 Heat 2 tablespoons of the olive oil in a large frying pan and cook the aubergine slices for 2–3 minutes until just beginning to brown. Remove from the pan. Add the rest of the oil to the pan and cook the courgette slices until browned.

3 Lay half of the aubergine slices in the base of an ovenproof dish. Cover with half of the tomato sauce and then add a layer of courgettes. Top with half of the mozzarella slices.

4 Repeat the layers and bake in a pre-heated oven, at 180°C/350°F/Gas Mark 4, for 45–50 minutes or until the vegetables are tender. Garnish with fresh basil leaves and serve immediately.

rice with fruit & nuts

*Here is a filling, spicy rice dish that includes fruits for a
refreshing flavour and toasted nuts for a crunchy texture.*

Preparation time 20 mins
Cooking time 1 hour
Serves 6

Calories 423
Carbohydrate 62 g
Sugars 19 g
Protein 10 g
Fat 17 g
Saturates 2 g

INGREDIENTS

4 tbsp vegetable ghee or vegetable oil

1 large onion, chopped

2 garlic cloves, crushed

2.5-cm/1-inch piece root
   ginger, chopped

1 tsp chilli powder

1 tsp cumin seeds

1 tbsp mild or medium curry powder
   or paste

300 g/10½ oz brown rice

850 ml/1½ pints boiling vegetable stock

400 g/14 oz canned chopped tomatoes

175 g/6 oz ready-to-eat dried apricots or
   peaches, cut into slivers

1 red pepper, deseeded and diced

85 g/3 oz frozen peas

1–2 small, slightly green bananas

55–85 g/2–3 oz toasted nuts, such as
   almonds, cashews, hazelnuts or
   pine kernels

salt and pepper

sprigs of fresh coriander, to garnish

1   Heat the ghee or oil in a large pan. Add the onion and cook over a low heat
for 3 minutes. Stir in the garlic, ginger, spices and rice and cook gently, stirring
constantly, for 2 minutes, until the rice is coated in the spiced oil.

2   Pour in the boiling stock, add the chopped tomatoes and season. Bring to the
boil, then reduce the heat, cover and simmer gently for 40 minutes or until the rice
is almost cooked and most of the liquid has been absorbed.

3   Add the apricots or peaches, diced red pepper and peas. Cover and cook for
10 minutes. Remove from the heat and set aside for 5 minutes without uncovering.

4   Peel and slice the bananas. Uncover the rice mixture and fork through to mix the
ingredients and fluff up the rice. Add the toasted nuts and sliced bananas and toss
together lightly. Transfer to a warmed serving platter and then garnish with the fresh
coriander sprigs. Serve immediately.

ratatouille grill

Ratatouille is a classic French dish of vegetables cooked in a tomato and herb sauce. Here it is topped with diced potatoes and a golden layer of cheese.

Preparation time 15 mins
Cooking time 25 mins
Serves 4

Calories 287
Carbohydrate 53 g
Sugars 13 g
Protein 14 g
Fat 4 g
Saturates 2 g

INGREDIENTS

2 onions

1 garlic clove

1 red pepper

1 green pepper

1 aubergine

2 courgettes

800 g/1 lb 12 oz canned
    chopped tomatoes

1 bouquet garni

2 tbsp tomato purée

900 g/2 lb potatoes

75 g/2¾ oz reduced-fat mature Cheddar
    cheese, grated

salt and pepper

2 tbsp snipped fresh chives, to garnish

1   Peel and finely chop the onions and garlic. Rinse, deseed and slice the peppers. Rinse, trim and cut the aubergine into small cubes. Rinse, trim and thinly slice the courgettes.

2   Place the onion, garlic and peppers into a large saucepan. Add the tomatoes, and stir in the bouquet garni, tomato purée and salt and pepper to taste. Bring to the boil, cover and simmer for 10 minutes, stirring half-way through. Stir in the prepared aubergine and courgettes and cook, uncovered, for a further 10 minutes, stirring occasionally.

3   Meanwhile, peel the potatoes and cut into 2.5-cm/1-inch cubes. Place the potatoes in another saucepan and cover with water. Bring to the boil and cook for 10–12 minutes until tender. Drain and set aside.

4   Transfer the vegetables to a heatproof gratin dish. Arrange the cooked potatoes evenly over the vegetables.

5   Pre-heat the grill to medium. Sprinkle grated cheese over the potatoes and place under the grill for 5 minutes until golden, bubbling and hot. Serve garnished with snipped chives.

linguine with pesto sauce

The basil, olive oil, garlic and pine kernels in this traditional
pasta sauce are the essence of Italian cooking.

Preparation time 15 mins
Cooking time 10–15 mins
Serves 4

Calories 860
Sugars 4 g
Protein 30 g
Fat 50 g
Carbohydrate 77 g
Saturates 12 g

INGREDIENTS
400 g/14 oz dried or fresh linguine
freshly grated Parmesan cheese,
   to serve (optional)
PESTO SAUCE
150 g/5½ oz Parmesan cheese in
   a wedge
3 garlic cloves, or to taste
150 g/5½ oz fresh basil leaves
5 tbsp pine kernels
150 ml/5 fl oz extra-virgin olive oil
salt and pepper

1 To make the pesto sauce, cut the rind off the Parmesan and finely grate the cheese. Set aside. Cut each garlic clove in half lengthways and use the tip of the knife to lift out the green core, which can have a bitter flavour if the cloves are old. Coarsely chop the garlic.

2 Rinse the basil leaves and pat dry with kitchen paper. Put the basil in a food processor and add the pine kernels, grated cheese, chopped garlic and olive oil. Process for about 30 seconds, just until blended.

3 Add pepper and extra salt to taste, but remember the cheese is already salty. Cover with a sheet of clingfilm and chill for up to 5 days.

4 Bring a large pan of water to the boil. Add ½ teaspoon salt and the linguine and cook according to the packet instructions until just tender, but still firm to the bite. Drain well, reserving a little of the cooking water.

5 Return the linguine to the pan over a low heat and stir in the sauce. Toss until the pasta is well coated and the sauce is heated though. Stir in about 2 tablespoons of the reserved cooking water if the sauce seems too thick.

6 Serve at once, with grated Parmesan.

spinach & cheese curry

This vegetarian curry is full of protein and iron.

Preparation time 20–30 mins

Cooking time 25 mins

Serves 4

Calories 578

Carbohydrate 4 g

Sugars 4 g

Protein 10 g

Fat 58 g

Saturates 7 g

INGREDIENTS

300 ml/10 fl oz vegetable oil

200 g/7 oz paneer cheese, cubed

3 tomatoes, sliced

1 tsp ground cumin

1½ tsp chilli powder

1 tsp salt

400 g/14 oz spinach

3 green chillies

pooris or boiled rice, to serve

1 Heat the vegetable oil in a large, heavy-based frying pan. Add the cubed paneer and fry, stirring occasionally, until it is golden brown.

2 Add the tomatoes to the pan then stir in the ground cumin, chilli powder and salt and stir-fry for 2 minutes.

3 Add the spinach leaves to the pan and stir-fry over a low heat for about 7–10 minutes until wilted.

4 Add the green chillies and cook, stirring constantly, for a further 2 minutes.

5 Transfer to warmed serving plates and serve immediately with pooris or plain boiled rice.

mooli curry

This is a rather unusual recipe for a vegetarian curry using mooli,

a long white radish. The dish is good served hot with chapatis.

Preparation time 10 mins
Cooking time 20 mins
Serves 4

Calories 384
Carbohydrate 9 g
Sugars 4 g
Protein 3 g
Fat 38 g
Saturates 4 g

INGREDIENTS

500 g/1 lb 2 oz mooli, preferably
   with leaves

1 tbsp moong dhal

600 ml/1 pint water

150 ml/5 fl oz vegetable oil

1 medium onion, thinly sliced

1 tsp crushed garlic

1 tsp chilli flakes

1 tsp salt

chapatis, to serve

1 Rinse, peel and roughly slice the mooli, with its leaves, if using.

2 Place the mooli, the leaves, if using, and the moong dhal in a large saucepan and pour over the water. Bring to the boil and cook over a medium heat until the mooli has softened. Drain the mooli mixture thoroughly and squeeze out any excess water, using your hands.

3 Heat the vegetable oil in a heavy-based saucepan. Add the onion, garlic, chilli flakes and salt and fry over a medium

heat, stirring from time to time, for 5–7 minutes, until the onions are light golden.

4 Stir the mooli mixture into the spiced onion mixture and combine well. Reduce the heat and continue cooking, stirring frequently, for 3–5 minutes.

5 Transfer the mooli curry to individual warmed serving plates and serve hot with chapatis.

potato curry

Served hot with pooris, this curry makes an excellent lunch dish with mango chutney as the perfect accompaniment.

Preparation time 10 mins
Cooking time 25 mins
Serves 4

Calories 390
Carbohydrate 19 g
Sugars 0.7 g
Protein 2 g
Fat 34 g
Saturates 4 g

INGREDIENTS

3 medium potatoes

150 ml/5 fl oz vegetable oil

1 tsp onion seeds

½ tsp fennel seeds

4 curry leaves

1 tsp ground cumin

1 tsp ground coriander

1 tsp chilli powder

pinch of turmeric

1 tsp salt

1½ tsp dried mango powder

1   Peel and rinse the potatoes. Using a sharp knife, cut each potato into 6 slices. Cook the potato slices in a saucepan of boiling water until just cooked, but not mushy (test by piercing with a sharp knife or a skewer). Drain and set aside until required.

2   Heat the vegetable oil in a separate, heavy-based saucepan over a moderate heat. Reduce the heat and add the onion seeds and fennel seeds.

3   Add the curry leaves and stir thoroughly. Remove the pan from the heat and add the ground cumin, coriander, chilli powder, turmeric, salt and dried mango powder, stirring well to combine.

4   Return the pan to a low heat and fry the mixture, stirring constantly, for about 1 minute.

5   Pour this mixture over the cooked potatoes, mix together and stir-fry over a low heat for about 5 minutes.

6   Transfer the potato curry to serving dishes and serve.

chick pea curry

This curry is very popular in India. There are many different ways of cooking chick peas, but this version is probably one of the most delicious.

Preparation time 5–10 mins
Cooking time 15 mins
Serves 4

Calories 114
Carbohydrate 10.1 g
Sugars 1.9 g
Protein 2.9 g
Fat 7.3 g
Saturates 0.7 g

INGREDIENTS

6 tbsp vegetable oil

2 onions, sliced

1 tsp finely chopped root ginger

1 tsp ground cumin

1 tsp ground coriander

1 tsp crushed fresh garlic

1 tsp chilli powder

2 green chillies

1 tbsp fresh coriander leaves

150 ml/5 fl oz water

300 g/10 oz potatoes

400 g/14 oz canned chick peas, drained

1 tbsp lemon juice

1 Heat the oil in a large saucepan over a medium heat. Add the onions to the pan and fry, stirring occasionally, until they are golden brown.

2 Reduce the heat, add the ginger, ground cumin, ground coriander, garlic, chilli powder, green chillies and fresh coriander leaves to the pan and stir-fry for 2 minutes. Add the water to the pan and stir to mix.

3 Using a sharp knife, cut the potatoes into small cubes.

4 Add the potatoes and the drained chick peas to the mixture in the pan, cover and leave to simmer, stirring occasionally, for 5–7 minutes.

5 Sprinkle the lemon juice over the curry.

6 Transfer the chick pea curry to serving dishes and serve.

egg curry

This curry can be made very quickly. It can either be served as a side dish or, with parathas, as a light lunch.

Preparation time 10 mins
Cooking time 15 mins
Serves 4

Calories 189
Carbohydrate 4 g
Sugars 3 g
Protein 7 g
Fat 16 g
Saturates 3 g

INGREDIENTS

4 tbsp vegetable oil

1 medium onion, sliced

1 fresh red chilli, finely chopped

½ tsp chilli powder

½ tsp finely chopped root ginger

½ tsp crushed fresh garlic

4 medium eggs

1 firm tomato, sliced

fresh coriander leaves

parathas, to serve (optional)

1 Heat the oil in a large, heavy-based saucepan. Add the sliced onion to the pan and fry over a medium heat, stirring occasionally, for about 5 minutes, until it is just softened and a light golden colour.

2 Lower the heat. Add the fresh red chilli, the chilli powder, the chopped ginger and the crushed garlic to the pan and fry over a low heat, stirring constantly, for about 1 minute.

3 Add the eggs and tomato to the pan and continue cooking, stirring to break up the eggs when they begin to cook, for a further 3–5 minutes.

4 Sprinkle the fresh coriander leaves over the curry and transfer it to warm serving plates.

5 Serve the egg curry immediately, with parathas to accompany it, if you wish.

potato & cauliflower curry

Potatoes and cauliflower go very well together. Served with
dhaal and pooris, this dish makes a perfect vegetarian meal.

Preparation time 10 mins
Cooking time 25 mins
Serves 4

Calories 426
Carbohydrate 26 g
Sugars 6 g
Protein 4 g
Fat 35 g
Saturates 4 g

INGREDIENTS

150 ml/5 fl oz oil

½ tsp white cumin seeds

4 dried red chillies

2 medium onions, sliced

1 tsp finely chopped root ginger

1 tsp crushed fresh garlic

1 tsp chilli powder

1 tsp salt

pinch of turmeric

3 medium potatoes

½ cauliflower, cut into small florets

2 green chillies (optional)

small handful of fresh
   coriander leaves

150 ml/5 fl oz pint water

1   Heat the oil in a large saucepan.

2   Add the white cumin seeds and dried red chillies to the pan, stirring to mix.

3   Add the onions to the pan and fry, stirring occasionally, until golden brown.

4   Add the ginger, garlic, chilli powder, salt and turmeric to the onions and stir-fry
for about 2 minutes.

5   Add the potatoes and cauliflower to the onion and spice mixture, stirring to coat
the vegetables in the spice mixture.

6   Reduce the heat and add the green chillies (if using), fresh coriander leaves and
water to the pan. Cover and leave the mixture to simmer for 10–15 minutes.

7   Transfer the potato and cauliflower curry to warm serving plates and serve.

potato & mixed fish soup

*Any mixture of fish is suitable for this recipe, from simple smoked
and white fish to salmon or mussels, depending on the occasion.*

Preparation time 10 mins
Cooking time 35 mins
Serves 4

Calories 458
Carbohydrate 22 g
Sugars 5 g
Protein 28 g
Fat 25 g
Saturates 12 g

INGREDIENTS

2 tbsp vegetable oil

450 g/1 lb small new potatoes, halved

1 bunch spring onions, sliced

1 yellow pepper, sliced

2 garlic cloves, crushed

225 ml/8 fl oz dry white wine

600 ml/1 pint fish stock

225 g/8 oz white fish fillet, skinned
    and cubed

225 g/8 oz smoked cod fillet, skinned
    and cubed

2 tomatoes, skinned, deseeded
    and chopped

100 g/3½ oz peeled cooked prawns

150 ml/5 fl oz pint double cream

2 tbsp shredded fresh basil

1   Heat the vegetable oil in a large saucepan and add the
potatoes, sliced spring onions, pepper and garlic. Sauté
gently for 3 minutes, stirring constantly.

2   Add the white wine and fish stock to the saucepan and
bring to the boil. Reduce the heat and simmer the mixture

for 10–15 minutes. Add the cubed fish fillets and the
tomatoes to the soup and continue to cook gently for
10 minutes or until the fish is cooked through.

3   Stir in the prawns, cream and shredded basil and cook for
2–3 minutes. Pour the soup into warmed bowls and serve.

clam & sorrel soup

This recipe is intended to be served in small quantities, because the soup is very rich and full of flavour.

Preparation time 10-15 mins
Cooking time 30 mins
Serves 4

Calories 384
Carbohydrate 7 g
Sugars 4 g
Protein 18 g
Fat 29 g
Saturates 18 g

INGREDIENTS

900 g/2 lb live clams, scrubbed

1 onion, finely chopped

150 ml/5 fl oz dry white wine

50 g/1¾ oz butter

1 small carrot, finely diced

2 shallots, finely diced

1 celery stick, finely diced

2 bay leaves

150 ml/5 fl oz double cream

25 g/1 oz sorrel, shredded

pepper

dill, to garnish

crusty bread, to serve

1 Put the clams into a large saucepan with the onion and wine. Cover and cook over a high heat for 3–4 minutes until the clams have opened. Strain, reserving the cooking liquid, and discard the onion. Set aside the clams until they are cool enough to handle.

2 In a clean saucepan, melt the butter over a low heat. Add the carrot, shallots and celery and cook very gently for 10 minutes until softened but not coloured. Add the reserved cooking liquid and bay leaves and simmer the soup for a further 10 minutes.

3 Meanwhile, roughly chop the clams, if large. Add to the soup with the cream and sorrel. Simmer for a further 2–3 minutes until the sorrel has wilted. Season with pepper, garnish with dill and serve at once with crusty bread.

fish & crab chowder

Packed full of flavour, this delicious fish dish is really a meal in itself, but it is ideal accompanied by a crisp side salad.

Preparation time 40 mins
Cooking time 25 mins
Serves 4

Calories 440
Carbohydrate 43 g
Sugars 10 g
Protein 49 g
Fat 7 g
Saturates 1 g

INGREDIENTS

1 large onion, finely chopped
2 celery sticks, finely chopped
150 ml/5 fl oz dry white wine
600 ml/1 pint fish stock
600 ml/1 pint skimmed milk
1 bay leaf
225 g/8 oz smoked cod fillet, skinned
    and cut into 2.5-cm/1-inch cubes
225 g/8 oz smoked haddock fillets,
    skinned and cut into 2.5-cm/
    1-inch cubes
350g/12 oz canned crab meat, drained
225 g/8 oz French beans, blanched and
    sliced into 2.5-cm/1-inch pieces
225 g/8 oz cooked brown rice
4 tsp cornflour mixed with 4 tbsp water
salt and pepper
chopped fresh parsley, to garnish
mixed green salad, to serve

1 Place the onion, celery and wine in a large, non-stick saucepan. Bring to the boil, cover and cook over a low heat for 5 minutes. Uncover the pan and cook for a further 5 minutes until almost all the liquid has evaporated.

2 Pour in the stock and milk and add the bay leaf. Bring to a simmer and stir in the cod and haddock. Simmer over a low heat, uncovered, for 5 minutes.

3 Add the crab meat, beans and cooked brown rice and simmer gently for 2–3 minutes until just heated through. Discard the bay leaf.

4 Stir in the cornflour mixture and simmer gently until thickened slightly. Season to taste with salt and pepper and ladle into warmed soup bowls. Garnish with chopped parsley and serve with a mixed salad.

giant garlic prawns

In Spain, giant garlic prawns are cooked in small half-glazed earthenware dishes called cazuelas. The prawns arrive at your table sizzling.

Preparation time 5 mins
Cooking time 5–8 mins
Serves 4

Calories 385
Carbohydrate 1 g
Sugars 0 g
Protein 26 g
Fat 31 g
Saturates 5 g

INGREDIENTS

125 ml/4 fl oz olive oil

4 garlic cloves, finely chopped

2 hot red chillies, deseeded and
   finely chopped

450 g/1 lb cooked king prawns

2 tbsp chopped fresh flat–leaved parsley

salt and pepper

wedges of lemon, to garnish

crusty bread, to serve

1 Heat the olive oil in a large, heavy-based frying pan over a low heat. Add the garlic and chillies and cook, stirring occasionally, for 1–2 minutes until softened but not coloured.

2 Add the prawns and stir-fry for 2–3 minutes until heated through and coated in the oil and garlic mixture.

3 Turn off the heat and add the chopped parsley, stirring well to mix. Season to taste with salt and pepper.

4 Divide the prawns and garlic-flavoured oil between warmed serving dishes, garnish with lemon wedges and serve with lots of crusty bread.

rice with seafood

This soup-like main course rice dish is packed with a tempting array of fresh seafood and is typically Thai in flavour.

Preparation time 5–10 mins

Cooking time 20 mins

Serves 4

Calories 370

Carbohydrate 52 g

Sugars 0 g

Protein 27 g

Fat 8 g

Saturates 1 g

INGREDIENTS

12 live mussels, scrubbed and bearded

2 litres/3½ pints fish stock

2 tbsp vegetable oil

1 garlic clove, crushed

1 tsp grated root ginger

1 fresh red bird's-eye chilli, chopped

2 spring onions, chopped

225 g/8 oz long-grain rice

2 small squid, cleaned and sliced

100 g/3½ oz firm white fish fillet, such as
   halibut or monkfish, cut into chunks

100 g/3½ oz raw prawns, peeled

2 tbsp Thai fish sauce

3 tbsp chopped fresh coriander

1 Discard any mussels with damaged shells or open ones that do not close when firmly tapped with a knife. Pour 4 tablespoons of the stock into a large pan. Add the mussels, cover and cook over a medium heat, shaking the pan until the mussels open. Remove from the heat and discard any that do not open.

2 Heat the oil in a large frying pan or wok and fry the garlic, ginger, chilli and spring onions for 30 seconds. Add the remaining stock and bring to the boil.

3 Stir in the rice, then add the squid, fish chunks and prawns. Lower the heat and simmer gently for 15 minutes or until the rice is cooked. Add the fish sauce and mussels.

4 Ladle into wide bowls and sprinkle with coriander.

spicy monkfish rice

A Thai-influenced dish of rice, cooked in coconut milk, with spicy
grilled monkfish and fresh peas – what could be better?

Preparation time 30 mins
Cooking time 30 mins
Serves 4

Calories 440
Carbohydrate 60 g
Sugars 8 g
Protein 22 g
Fat 14 g
Saturates 2 g

INGREDIENTS

1 hot red chilli, deseeded
  and chopped

1 tsp chilli flakes

2 garlic cloves, chopped

pinch of saffron

3 tbsp roughly chopped fresh
  mint leaves

4 tbsp olive oil

2 tbsp lemon juice

375 g/12 oz monkfish fillet, cut
  into bite-sized pieces

1 onion, finely chopped

225 g/8 oz long grain rice

400g/14 oz canned chopped tomatoes

200 ml/7 fl oz coconut milk

115 g/4 oz peas

salt and pepper

2 tbsp chopped fresh coriander,
  to garnish

1   Process the chilli, chill flakes, garlic, saffron, mint, olive oil and lemon juice in a
food processor or blender until combined, but not smooth.

2   Put the monkfish into a non-metallic dish and pour over the spice paste, turning
to coat. Cover and set aside for 20 minutes to marinate.

3   Heat a large pan until very hot. Using a draining spoon, lift the monkfish from the
marinade and add, in batches, to the hot pan. Cook for 3–4 minutes until browned
and firm. Remove with a slotted spoon and set aside.

4   Add the onion and remaining marinade to the pan and cook for 5 minutes until
softened and lightly browned. Add the rice and stir until well coated. Add the
tomatoes and coconut milk. Bring to the boil, cover and simmer very gently for
15 minutes. Stir in the peas, season and arrange the fish over the top. Cover with
foil and continue to cook over a very low heat for 5 minutes. Serve garnished with
the chopped coriander.

prawns in green sauce

The sweet briny flesh of prawns is wonderful paired with the smoky flavour of chipotle chillies.

Preparation time 10 mins
Cooking time 15–20 mins
Serves 4

Calories 225
Carbohydrate 17 g
Sugars 13 g
Protein 24 g
Fat 8 g
Saturates 1 g

INGREDIENTS

2 tbsp vegetable oil

3 onions, chopped

5 garlic cloves, chopped

5–7 ripe tomatoes, diced

175–225 g/6–8 oz French beans, cut into
   5-cm/2-inch pieces and blanched for
   1 minute

¼ tsp ground cumin

pinch of ground allspice

pinch of ground cinnamon

½–1 canned chipotle chilli in adobo
   marinade, with some of the marinade

450 ml/16 fl oz fish stock or water mixed
   with a fish stock cube

450 g/1 lb raw prawns, peeled

sprigs of fresh coriander, to garnish

1 lime, cut into wedges, to serve

1 Heat the oil in a large pan. Add the onions and garlic and cook over a low heat, stirring occasionally, for 5–10 minutes until softened. Add the tomatoes and cook for 2 minutes.

2 Add the blanched French beans, cumin, allspice, cinnamon, chipotle chilli and marinade and fish stock. Bring to the boil, then reduce the heat and simmer for a few minutes to combine the flavours.

3 Add the prawns and cook, stirring gently, for 1–2 minutes only, then remove the pan from the heat and set the prawns aside to steep in the hot liquid to finish cooking. They are cooked when they have turned a bright pink colour.

4 Serve the prawns immediately, garnished with the fresh coriander and accompanied by the lime wedges.

modern kedgeree

This is a modern version of the classic dish, using smoked salmon as well as fresh salmon and lots of fresh dill – perfect for a dinner party.

Preparation time 10 mins
Cooking time 35 mins
Serves 6

Calories 370
Carbohydrate 39 g
Sugars 3 g
Protein 10 g
Fat 19 g
Saturates 9 g

INGREDIENTS

2 g/1 oz butter

1 tbsp olive oil

1 onion, finely chopped

1 garlic clove, finely chopped

175 g/6 oz long-grain rice

400 ml/14 fl oz fish stock

175 g/6 oz salmon fillet, skinned
   and chopped

85 g/3 oz smoked salmon, chopped

2 tbsp double cream

2 tbsp chopped fresh dill

3 spring onions, finely chopped

salt and pepper

sprigs of fresh dill and slices of lemon,
   to garnish

1 Melt the butter with the oil in a large saucepan. Add the onion and cook over a low heat for 10 minutes until softened, but not coloured. Add the garlic and cook for a further 30 seconds.

2 Add the rice and cook for 2–3 minutes, stirring constantly, until transparent. Add the fish stock and stir well. Bring to the boil, cover and simmer very gently for 10 minutes.

3 Add the salmon fillet and the smoked salmon and stir well, adding a little more stock or water if the mixture seems dry. Cook for a further 6–8 minutes until the fish and rice are tender and all the stock is absorbed.

4 Turn off the heat and stir in the cream, chopped dill and spring onions. Season to taste with salt and pepper and serve, garnished with sprigs of fresh dill and slices of lemon.

jambalaya

Jambalaya is a dish of Cajun origin. There are as many versions of this dish as there are people who cook it. Here is a straightforward one.

Preparation time 10 mins
Cooking time 45 mins
Serves 4

Calories 283
Carbohydrate 12 g
Sugars 8 g
Protein 30 g
Fat 14 g
Saturates 3 g

INGREDIENTS

2 tbsp vegetable oil

2 onions, roughly chopped

1 green pepper, deseeded and
   roughly chopped

2 celery sticks, roughly chopped

3 garlic cloves, finely chopped

2 tsp paprika

300 g/10 oz skinless, boneless chicken
   breasts, chopped

100 g/3½ oz kabanos sausages, chopped

3 tomatoes, peeled and chopped

450 g/1 lb long-grain rice

850 ml/1½ pint hot chicken or fish stock

1 tsp dried oregano

2 bay leaves

12 large prawn tails

4 spring onions, finely chopped

2 tbsp chopped fresh parsley

salt and pepper

salad, to serve

1 Heat the vegetable oil in a large frying pan and add the onions, pepper, celery and garlic. Cook over a low heat, stirring occasionally, for 8–10 minutes until all the vegetables have softened. Add the paprika and cook for a further 30 seconds. Add the chicken and sausages and cook for 8–10 minutes until lightly browned. Add the tomatoes and cook for 2–3 minutes until broken up.

2 Add the rice to the pan and stir well. Pour in the hot stock and stir in the oregano and bay leaves. Cover and simmer for 10 minutes over a very low heat.

3 Add the prawns and stir well. Cover again and cook for a further 6–8 minutes until the rice is tender and the prawns are cooked through.

4 Stir in the spring onions and parsley and season to taste. Serve with salad.

italian fish stew

This robust stew is full of Mediterranean flavours. If you do not want to prepare the fish yourself, ask your local fishmonger to do it for you.

Preparation time 5–10 mins
Cooking time 25 mins
Serves 4

Calories 236
Carbohydrate 25 g
Sugars 4 g
Protein 20 g
Fat 7 g
Saturates 1 g

INGREDIENTS

2 tbsp olive oil

2 red onions, finely chopped

1 garlic clove, crushed

2 courgettes, sliced

400 g/14 oz canned chopped tomatoes

850 ml/1½ pints fish or vegetable stock

85 g/3 oz dried short pasta, such
   as conchiglie

350 g/12 oz firm white fish, such as cod,
   haddock or hake

1 tbsp chopped fresh basil or oregano,
   or 1 tsp dried oregano

1 tsp grated lemon rind

1 tbsp cornflour

1 tbsp water

salt and pepper

sprigs of fresh basil or oregano,
   to garnish

1 Heat the oil in a large pan. Add the onions and garlic and cook over a low heat, stirring occasionally, for about 5 minutes until softened. Add the courgettes and cook, stirring frequently, for 2–3 minutes.

2 Add the tomatoes and stock to the pan and bring to the boil. Add the pasta, bring back to the boil, reduce the heat and cover. Simmer for 8 minutes.

3 Skin and bone the fish, then cut it into chunks. Add to the pan with the basil or oregano and lemon rind and simmer gently for 5 minutes until the fish is opaque and flakes easily (take care not to overcook it) and the pasta is just tender, but still firm to the bite.

4 Blend the cornflour with the water to a smooth paste and stir into the stew. Cook gently for 2 minutes, stirring constantly, until thickened. Season with salt and pepper to taste.

5 Ladle the stew into 4 warmed soup bowls. Garnish with basil or oregano sprigs and serve immediately.

squid stew

This is a rich and flavoursome stew of slowly cooked squid, in a sauce
of tomatoes and red wine. The squid becomes very tender.

Preparation time 20 mins
Cooking time 2¼ hours
Serves 4

Calories 284
Carbohydrate 9 g
Sugars 5 g
Protein 31 g
Fat 12 g
Saturates 2 g

INGREDIENTS

750 g/1 lb 10 oz whole squid

3 tbsp olive oil

1 onion, chopped

3 garlic cloves, finely chopped

1 tsp fresh thyme leaves

400 g/14 oz canned chopped tomatoes

150 ml/5 fl oz red wine

300 ml/10 fl oz water

1 tbsp chopped fresh parsley

salt and pepper

1 To prepare whole squid, hold the body firmly and grasp the tentacles just inside the body. Pull firmly to remove the innards. Find the transparent 'quill' and remove. Grasp the wings on the outside of the body and pull to remove the outer skin. Trim the tentacles just below the beak and reserve. Wash the body and tentacles under cold running water. Slice the body into rings. Drain well on kitchen paper.

2 Heat the oil in a large, flameproof casserole. Add the prepared squid and cook over a medium heat, stirring occasionally, until lightly browned. Reduce the heat and add the onion, garlic and thyme. Cook for a further 5 minutes until softened.

3 Stir in the canned tomatoes, red wine and water. Bring to the boil and cook in a pre-heated oven, at 140°C/275°F/ Gas Mark 1, for 2 hours. Stir in the parsley and season to taste. Serve immediately.

cod curry

Using curry paste in this recipe makes it quick and easy to prepare. It makes an ideal family supper.

Preparation time 10 mins
Cooking time 25 mins
Serves 4

Calories 310
Carbohydrate 19 g
Sugars 4 g
Protein 42 g
Fat 8 g
Saturates 1 g

INGREDIENTS

1 tbsp vegetable oil

1 small onion, chopped

2 garlic cloves, chopped

2.5-cm/1-inch piece root ginger,
   roughly chopped

2 large ripe tomatoes, peeled and
   roughly chopped

150 ml/5 fl oz fish stock

1 tbsp medium curry paste

1 tsp ground coriander

400 g/14 oz canned chick peas, drained
   and rinsed

750 g/1 lb 10 oz cod fillet, cut into
   large chunks

4 tbsp chopped fresh coriander

4 tbsp thick yogurt

salt and pepper

steamed basmati rice, to serve

1 Heat the oil in a large pan and add the onion, garlic and ginger. Cook over a low heat for 4–5 minutes until softened. Remove from the heat. Put the onion mixture into a food processor or blender with the tomatoes and fish stock and process until smooth.

2 Return to the pan with the curry paste, ground coriander and chick peas. Mix together well, then simmer gently for 15 minutes until thickened.

3 Add the pieces of fish and return to a simmer. Cook for 5 minutes until the fish is just tender. Remove from the heat and set aside for 2–3 minutes.

4 Stir in the coriander and yogurt. Season and serve with basmati rice.

fish & rice with dark rum

*Based on a traditional Cuban recipe, this dish is similar to
Spanish paella, but it has the added kick of dark rum.*

Preparation time 2¼ hours
Cooking time 35 mins
Serves 4

Calories 547
Carbohydrate 85 g
Sugars 9 g
Protein 27 g
Fat 4 g
Saturates 1 g

INGREDIENTS

450 g/1 lb firm white fish fillets (such as
    cod or monkfish), skinned and cut into
    2.5-cm/1-inch cubes

2 tsp ground cumin

2 tsp dried oregano

2 tbsp lime juice

150 ml/5 fl oz dark rum

1 tbsp dark muscovado sugar

salt and pepper

3 garlic cloves, finely chopped

1 large onion, chopped

1 red pepper, deseeded and sliced
    into rings

1 green pepper, deseeded and sliced
    into rings

1 yellow pepper, deseeded and sliced
    into rings

1.2 litres/2 pints fish stock

350 g/12 oz long-grain rice

crusty bread, to serve

TO GARNISH

fresh oregano leaves

wedges of lime

1 Place the cubes of fish in a bowl and add the cumin, oregano, lime juice, rum and sugar. Season to taste with salt and pepper. Mix thoroughly, cover with clingfilm and set aside to chill for 2 hours.

2 Meanwhile, place the garlic, onion and peppers in a large pan. Pour in the stock and stir in the rice. Bring to the boil, lower the heat, cover and simmer for 15 minutes.

3 Gently stir in the fish and the marinade juices. Bring back to the boil and simmer, uncovered, stirring occasionally but taking care not to break up the fish, for about 5 minutes until the fish is cooked through and the rice is tender.

4 Season to taste with salt and pepper and transfer to a warmed serving plate. Garnish with fresh oregano and lime wedges and serve with crusty bread.

baked fresh sardines

Here, fresh sardines are baked with eggs, herbs and vegetables
to form a dish rather like an elaborate omelette.

Preparation time 35 mins
Cooking time 20–25 mins
Serves 4

Calories 690
Carbohydrate 17 g
Sugars 12 g
Protein 63 g
Fat 42 g
Saturates 15 g

INGREDIENTS

2 tbsp olive oil

2 large onions, sliced into rings

3 garlic cloves, chopped

2 large courgettes, cut into sticks

3 tbsp fresh thyme, stalks removed

8 large sardine fillets or 4 large
   sardines, filleted

115g/4oz grated Parmesan cheese

4 eggs, beaten

300 ml/10 fl oz milk

salt and pepper

1 Heat 1 tablespoon of the olive oil in a frying pan. Add the onion rings and chopped garlic and fry over a low heat, stirring occasionally, for 2–3 minutes until soft and translucent. Add the courgettes and cook, stirring occasionally, for about 5 minutes or until turning golden. Stir 2 tablespoons of the thyme leaves into the mixture and remove from the heat.

2 Place half of the onion and courgette mixture in the base of a large ovenproof dish.

3 Top with the sardine fillets and half the grated Parmesan cheese. Place the remaining onions and courgettes on top and sprinkle with the remaining thyme.

4 Mix the eggs and milk together in a bowl and season to taste with salt and pepper. Pour the mixture into the dish. Sprinkle the remaining Parmesan cheese over the top.

5 Bake in a pre-heated oven, at 180°C/350°F/Gas Mark 4, for 20–25 minutes, or until golden and set. Serve hot.

seafood risotto with oregano

The Genoese risotto is cooked in a different way from any of the other risottos. First, you cook the rice, then you prepare a sauce, then you mix the two together. The results are just as delicious, though!

Preparation time 10 mins
Cooking time 25 mins
Serves 4

Calories 424
Carbohydrate 46 g
Sugars 0 g
Protein 23 g
Fat 17 g
Saturates 10 g

INGREDIENTS

1.2 litres/2 pints hot fish or
   chicken stock

350 g/12 oz arborio rice, washed

50 g/1¾ oz butter

2 garlic cloves, chopped

250 g/9 oz mixed seafood, preferably
   raw, such as prawns, squid, mussels,
   clams and shrimps

2 tbsp chopped oregano, plus extra
   for garnishing

50 g/1¾ oz grated pecorino or Parmesan
   cheese, grated

1 In a large saucepan, bring the stock to the boil. Add the rice and cook for about 12 minutes, stirring, until the rice is tender, or follow the instructions on the packet. Drain thoroughly, reserving any excess liquid.

2 Heat the butter in a large frying pan and add the garlic, stirring. Add the mixed seafood to the pan and cook for 5 minutes if it is raw, and for 2–3 minutes if it is cooked. Stir in the oregano.

3 Add the cooked rice to the pan and cook for 2–3 minutes, stirring, or until hot. Add the reserved stock if the mixture gets too sticky.

4 Add the pecorino or Parmesan cheese and mix well.

5 Transfer the risotto to warm serving dishes and serve.

crab risotto

A different way to make the most of crab, this rich-tasting
and colourful risotto is full of interesting flavours.

Preparation time 15 mins
Cooking time 50 mins
Serves 4–6

Calories 447
Carbohydrate 62 g
Sugars 11 g
Protein 22 g
Fat 13 g
Saturates 2 g

INGREDIENTS

2–3 large red peppers

3 tbsp olive oil

1 onion, finely chopped

1 small bulb fennel, finely chopped

2 celery sticks, finely chopped

¼–½ tsp cayenne pepper

350 g/12 oz arborio or carnaroli rice

800 g/1 lb 12 oz canned tomatoes,
    drained and chopped

50 ml/2 fl oz dry white vermouth
    (optional)

1.5 litres/2¾ pints fish or chicken
    stock, simmering

450 g/1 lb freshly cooked crab meat

50 ml/2 fl oz lemon juice

2–4 tbsp chopped fresh parsley or chervil

salt and pepper

1 Grill the peppers until the skins are charred. Transfer to a plastic bag and twist to seal. When cool enough to handle, peel off the charred skins, working over a bowl to catch the juices. Remove the cores and seeds. Chop the flesh and set aside, reserving the juices.

2 Heat the olive oil in a large, heavy-based pan. Add the onion, fennel and celery and cook over a low heat, stirring occasionally, for 2–3 minutes until the vegetables are softened. Add the cayenne and rice and cook, stirring frequently, for about 2 minutes until the rice is translucent and well coated.

3 Stir in the chopped tomatoes and vermouth, if using. The liquid will bubble and steam rapidly. When the liquid is almost absorbed, add a ladleful (about 225 ml/ 8 fl oz) of the simmering stock. Cook, stirring constantly, until the liquid is completely absorbed.

4 Continue adding the stock, about half a ladleful at a time, allowing each addition to be absorbed before adding the next. This should take 20–25 minutes. The risotto should be creamy and the rice just tender, but still firm to the bite.

5 Stir in the red peppers and reserved juices, the crab meat, lemon juice and parsley or chervil and heat through. Season to taste. Serve immediately.

risotto with clams

This simple recipe is an excellent way of using the tiny Venus clams
when they are in season. The tomatoes add a splash of colour.

Preparation time 15 mins
Cooking time 40 mins
Serves 6

Calories 463
Carbohydrate 65 g
Sugars 4 g
Protein 25 g
Fat 12 g
Saturates 2 g

INGREDIENTS

50 ml/2 fl oz olive oil

1 large onion, finely chopped

2 kg/4 lb 8 oz tiny clams, such as Venus,
   well scrubbed

125 ml/4 fl oz dry white wine

1 litre/1¾ pints fish stock

600 ml/1 pint water

3 garlic cloves, finely chopped

½ tsp chilli flakes

400 g/14 oz arborio or carnaroli rice

3 ripe plum tomatoes, peeled and
   coarsely chopped

3 tbsp lemon juice

2 tbsp chopped fresh chervil or parsley

salt and pepper

1 Heat 1–2 tablespoons of the oil in a large, heavy-based pan over a medium-high heat. Add the onion and stir-fry for about 1 minute. Add the clams and wine and cover tightly. Cook for 2–3 minutes, shaking the pan frequently, until the clams begin to open. Remove from the heat and discard any clams that do not open.

2 When cool enough to handle, remove the clams from their shells. Rinse in the cooking liquid. Cover the clams and set aside. Strain the cooking liquid through a coffee filter or a sieve lined with kitchen paper and reserve.

3 Bring the fish stock and water to the boil in a pan, then reduce the heat and keep at a gentle simmer.

4 Heat the remaining olive oil in a large, heavy-based pan over a medium heat. Add the garlic and chilli flakes and cook gently for 1 minute. Add the rice and cook, stirring frequently, for about 2 minutes until translucent and well coated with oil.

5 Add a ladleful (about 225 ml/8 fl oz) of the simmering stock mixture; it will bubble and steam rapidly. Cook, stirring constantly, until the liquid is completely absorbed.

6 Continue adding the stock, about half a ladleful at a time, allowing each addition to be absorbed before adding the next – never allow the rice to cook 'dry'. This should take 20–25 minutes. The risotto should have a creamy consistency and the rice should be just tender, but still firm to the bite.

7 Stir in the tomatoes, reserved clams and their cooking liquid, the lemon juice and chervil or parsley. Heat through gently. Season to taste and serve.

lobster risotto

Although lobster is expensive, this dish is worth it. Keeping it simple allows the lobster flavour to come through.

Preparation time 10 mins
Cooking time 25 mins
Serves 4

Calories 688
Carbohydrate 69 g
Sugars 3 g
Protein 32 g
Fat 31 g
Saturates 16 g

INGREDIENTS

1 tbsp vegetable oil

4 tbsp unsalted butter

2 shallots, finely chopped

300 g/10½ oz arborio or carnaroli rice

½ tsp cayenne pepper

85 ml/3 fl oz dry white vermouth

1.5 litres/2¾ pints shellfish, fish or
   chicken stock, simmering

225 g/8 oz cherry tomatoes, quartered
   and deseeded

2–3 tbsp double or whipping cream

450 g/1 lb cooked lobster meat, cut into
   coarse chunks

2 tbsp chopped fresh chervil or dill

salt and white pepper

1 Heat the oil and half the butter in a large, heavy-based pan over a medium heat. Add the shallots and cook, stirring occasionally, for about 2 minutes until just beginning to soften. Add the rice and cayenne and cook, stirring frequently, for about 2 minutes until the rice is translucent and well coated with the oil and butter.

2 Pour in the vermouth; it will bubble and steam rapidly and evaporate almost immediately. Add a ladleful (about 225 ml/8 fl oz) of the simmering stock and cook, stirring constantly, until the stock is completely absorbed.

3 Continue adding the stock, about half a ladleful at a time, allowing each addition to be completely absorbed before adding the next – never allow the rice to cook 'dry'. This process should take about 20–25 minutes. The risotto should have a creamy consistency and the rice should be just tender, but still firm to the bite.

4 Stir in the tomatoes and cream and cook for about 2 minutes.

5 Add the cooked lobster meat with the remaining butter and chervil or dill and cook long enough to just heat the lobster meat gently. Serve immediately.

NOTE

This book uses imperial and metric measurements. Follow the same units
of measurement throughout; do not mix imperial and metric.
All spoon measurements are level: teaspoons are assumed to be 5 ml, and
tablespoons are assumed to be 15 ml. Unless otherwise stated,
milk is assumed to be whole, eggs and individual vegetables such as potatoes
are medium, and pepper is freshly ground black pepper.

The nutritional information provided for each recipe is per serving or per person.
Optional ingredients, variations, or serving suggestions have not been included in the calculations.
The times given for each recipe are an approximate guide only because the preparation times may
differ according to the techniques used by different people and the cooking times may
vary as a result of the type of oven used.

Recipes using raw or very lightly cooked eggs should be
avoided by infants, the elderly, pregnant women, convalescents,
and anyone suffering from an illness.